WHAT ARE FISH?

BOBI MARTIN

Britannica®
Educational Publishing

IN ASSOCIATION WITH

ROSEN
EDUCATIONAL SERVICES

Published in 2017 by Britannica Educational Publishing (a trademark of Encyclopædia Britannica, Inc.) in association with The Rosen Publishing Group, Inc.
29 East 21st Street, New York, NY 10010

Distributed exclusively by Rosen Publishing.
To see additional Britannica Educational Publishing titles, go to rosenpublishing.com.

First Edition

Britannica Educational Publishing
J.E. Luebering: Executive Director, Core Editorial
Mary Rose McCudden: Editor, Britannica Student Encyclopedia

Rosen Publishing
Bernadette Davis: Editor
Nelson Sá: Art Director
Brian Garvey: Designer
Cindy Reiman: Photography Manager
Nicole DiMella: Photo Researcher

Library of Congress Cataloging-in-Publication Data

Names: Martin, Bobi.
Title: What are fish? / Bobi Martin.
Description: First edition. | New York : Britannica Educational Publishing,
  2017. | Series: Let's find out! Marine life | Includes bibliographical
  references and index.
Identifiers: LCCN 2016029698 | ISBN 9781508103837 (library bound)
  | ISBN 9781508103844 (pbk.) | ISBN 9781508103127 (6-pack)
Subjects: LCSH: Fishes—Juvenile literature.
Classification: LCC QL617.2 .M343 2017 | DDC 597—dc23
LC record available at https://lccn.loc.gov/2016029698

Manufactured in China

Photo credits: Cover, p. 1, interior pages background image Leonardo Gonzalez/Shutterstock.com; p. 4 bluehand/Shutterstock.com; p. 5 Peter Green/Ardea Photographics; p. 6 © Richard Carey/Fotolia; p. 7 © Bryan and Cherry Alexander; pp. 8, 11, 12, 15, 16 Encyclopædia Britannica, Inc.; p. 9 Frederic Pacorel/The Image Bank/Getty Images; p. 10 © Dr. Richard L. Pyle and Dr. Brian D. Greene, 2007; p. 13 © tsrapp/Fotolia; pp. 14–15 Michael Weberberger/imageBROKER/Getty Images; pp. 16–17 Stephen Frink/Corbis Documentary/Getty Images; p. 18 Wolfgang Poelzer/WaterFrame/Getty Images; p. 19 kerkla/E+/Getty Images; p. 20 Roland Kilcher/Moment/Getty Images; p. 21 © Razvan Ciuca/Moment/Getty Images; p. 22 AppStock/Shutterstock.com; p. 23 Stephanie Howard/Moment Mobile/Getty Images; p. 24 U.S. Coast Guard; p. 25 Michael Patrick O'Neill/Science Source; p. 26 Jeffrey M. Frank/Shutterstock.com; p. 27 Evangelos/Shutterstock.com; pp. 28–29 Stuart Westmorland/Corbis Documentary/Getty Images; p. 29 © StrangerView/Fotolia.

CONTENTS

FISH ARE AMAZING!

Fish are a kind of animal that lives in water. They come in many sizes, shapes, and colors. Gobies, one of the smallest fish, are less than half an inch (13 millimeters) long. The whale shark, the largest fish, can be 59 feet (18 meters) long! Some fish are plain, while others, like

Gobies are one of the largest fish orders. There are more than 2,000 species!

Coelacanths (SEEL-uh-kanths) first appeared on Earth about 350 million years ago.

clownfish and lionfish, have bright colors and patterns. There are fish that look like plants, rocks, or snakes. There are fish that can change color and some that glow in the dark.

Fish live almost anywhere there is water, including rivers, lakes, and oceans. They are a major source of food for people and for other animals. Fish are the oldest known vertebrates—they have lived on Earth for more than 450 million years. There are more than thirty thousand species, or kinds, of fish. New ones are discovered every year!

VOCABULARY

Vertebrates are animals that have a backbone.

A Home Under Water

Fish live all around the world. Most fish are cold-blooded, which means they cannot make their own heat. Their bodies are the temperature of the water around them. Some fish live in warm tropical waters, while others live in icy Arctic seas.

Tropical fish, like these masked butterfly fish, prefer warmer waters.

When they are ready to reproduce, salmon migrate from the sea back to the same freshwater river where they were born.

Fish live in all kinds of water. Marine fish live in or near oceans, which have salt water. Freshwater fish live in lakes, rivers, or streams. Some fish, such as certain species of salmon and sturgeon, live most of their lives in salt water but migrate, or travel, to freshwater rivers to reproduce. No fish can live in water that is extremely salty. For instance, the Great Salt Lake in the United States and the Dead Sea in the Middle East contain so much salt that fish cannot live there.

THINK ABOUT IT

Fish are cold-blooded. In what ways is this helpful to them?

How Fish Breathe and Swim

Fish breathe through structures called gills. The gills allow fish to get oxygen from the water in the same way that lungs help people get oxygen from the air. Some fish also have simple lungs. These fish developed lungs to help them breathe when they have to be out of water for

A fish's gills allow oxygen in water to be absorbed into the fish's blood.

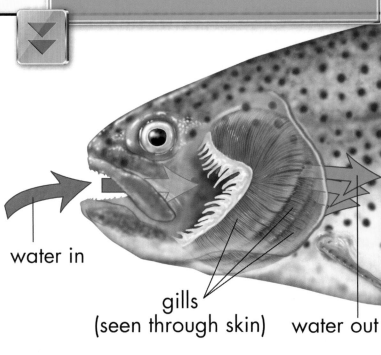

water in

gills
(seen through skin)   water out

COMPARE AND CONTRAST

Most fish use fins to turn and steer. Compare and contrast the way flying fish use their fins.

Flying fish propel themselves into the air at speeds up to 35 miles (56 kilometers) per hour!

a long time. Walking perch can survive on land for several days when they cross land to move from a pond that is drying up to a fuller pond.

Fish swim mainly by sideways movements of their body and tail. They use their fins to turn, steer, and brake. Some fish shoot a stream of water from their gills, which makes them lunge forward. Flying fish have large fins on their chest. When flying fish leap out of the water, their fins help them glide through the air.

What Do Fish Look Like?

A typical fish is narrower at the head and tail and wider in between. Nothing sticks out from the body except the fins, which can be pressed flat against the fish. A thin layer of slime also helps fish move quickly through water. A fish's shape is so good at allowing fish to move underwater that people patterned boats and submarines after this shape.

Most fish have scales that overlap each other, like

Ray-finned fishes use their spiny fins to protect themselves from predators.

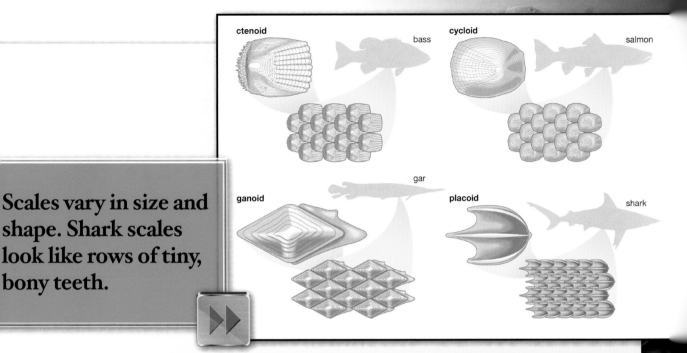

ctenoid — bass

cycloid — salmon

ganoid — gar

placoid — shark

Scales vary in size and shape. Shark scales look like rows of tiny, bony teeth.

▶▶

THINK ABOUT IT

Fish have scales that overlap. How does this help protect them?

shingles on a roof. Fish do not shed their scales like humans shed their hair, but if fish lose a scale, a new one grows in to take its place. As the fish grows, the scales also grow by adding rings of new material around the edge. An expert can tell the age of a fish by studying its scales. Unlike people, most fish keep growing as long as they live. Old fish may become very large.

Some Funny-Looking Fish

Some fish have unusual shapes. Seahorses have snouts like a horse and tails that curl around things. Leafy sea dragons are a type of seahorse that look like a leafy plant. Moray eels are long and slender—like snakes. The oarfish has a long, ribbon-like body that can be up to 50 feet

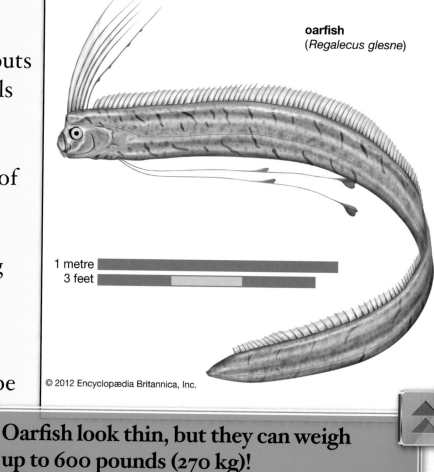

oarfish
(*Regalecus glesne*)

1 metre
3 feet

© 2012 Encyclopædia Britannica, Inc.

Oarfish look thin, but they can weigh up to 600 pounds (270 kg)!

COMPARE AND CONTRAST

Compare moray eels and oarfish. In what ways are they different?

(15 meters) long! A long, red fin runs along the oarfish's back and rises to a high crest on top of the head.

The rabbitfish, a small relative of sharks, has a head and teeth resembling a rabbit. Frogfish have bumpy bodies that blend into their surroundings of sponges and coral reefs. They use their fins to walk underwater. Some deep-water fish such as anglerfish and hatchetfish have adapted to their dark environment with body parts that glow!

A leafy sea dragon like this can be found in South Australia.

SHARKS!

Sharks are fish that have a skeleton made of **cartilage** instead of bone. Cartilage lets sharks bend and twist. It is lighter than bone, so this helps sharks swim fast. There are more than 400 species of sharks. Most sharks are smart and have well-developed senses. Many sharks can see well even in murky water, and some

dwarf lantern shark
(*Etmopterus perryi*)

Dwarf lantern sharks live in almost total darkness. Light from their bellies attracts prey.

sharks can detect prey using only their sense of smell. Most people are afraid of sharks, but only a few species are known to attack humans. Some sharks—including lemon, mako, and thrasher sharks—are considered valuable as food.

Sharks are among the oldest living things. They live in all the oceans of the world, even in the cold Arctic waters and the seas around Antarctica. The largest is the whale shark, which can grow up to 59 feet (18 meters) long and weigh 20 tons (18 metric tons). The smallest shark is the dwarf lantern shark, which is only about 7.5 inches (19 centimeters) long.

Hammerhead sharks rarely bother people. Their favorite food is the stingray.

WHAT DO FISH EAT?

Almost all fish eat other fish that are smaller than themselves. The smallest fish eat tiny water plants and animals called plankton. Freshwater fish may eat algae, plants, insects, frogs, and other fishes' larvae and eggs.

Sharks are at the top of the food chain in the ocean. Besides fish, some sharks eat seals, dolphins, squid, and

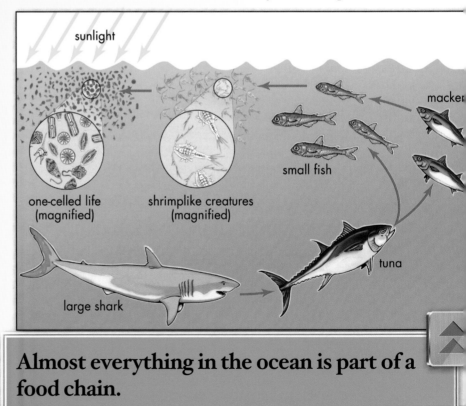

sunlight

one-celled life
(magnified)

shrimplike creatures
(magnified)

small fish

macker

tuna

large shark

Almost everything in the ocean is part of a food chain.

Like sharks, stingrays have cartilage instead of bones. This helps them be more flexible.

even sea turtles. Smaller fish feed on mollusks (including octopuses, shrimp, clams, and squid), sea stars, and other organisms that live in shallow water or in deeper water. Fish that live in the deepest part of the ocean cannot be picky. There is no light or plant life there. These fish feed on other deep-sea animals or on whatever scraps drift down to them.

THINK ABOUT IT
Different kinds of fish eat many different things. Why do you think this is?

THE LIFE CYCLE OF FISH

All fish hatch from eggs. Usually, females release eggs into the water and males fertilize them by releasing sperm. After a time, larvae hatch from the eggs. Soon, the larva forms a skeleton and develops fins and scales. Many eggs and larvae are eaten by other fish. Some kinds of fish try to protect

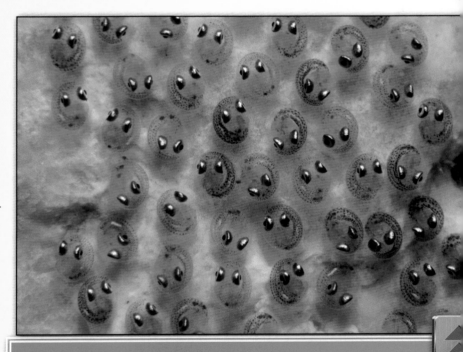

Most fish eggs are transparent, or see-through. A yolk sac provides food for the larvae after they hatch.

A female guppy may give birth to 60 or more live young at a time.

their eggs by hiding them, but most fish do not protect their eggs or their young. To increase the chance that some young will survive, a female releases hundreds, thousands, or even millions of eggs at a time. Sometimes the eggs are fertilized in the female's body and hatch there. The young are then born live from the female. Guppies, some sharks, and surfperches give birth to live young. After a fish grows into an adult, it will be ready to spawn.

VOCABULARY

Spawn means to produce young, especially in large numbers. Fish spawn by releasing eggs and sperm.

WHY WE NEED FISH

Fish are food for many animals. Bears, seals, and many birds consume fish as part of their diet. Fish are also an important source of food for humans. People all over the world eat many different kinds of fish, including cod, herring, and tuna.

Many bears eat fish as part of their diet.

COMPARE AND CONTRAST

Compare and contrast the ways that fish are important to people and to the environment.

In return for a safe home, clownfish help clean sea anemones.

Fish are also an important part of many ecosystems. Goby fish eat seaweeds that would kill coral reefs. Fish help control diseases such as malaria, yellow fever, and the zika virus by eating mosquito larvae. And through their waste products, fish provide nutrients that help plants grow. All of these things help keep ecosystems in balance. Additionally, researchers use some fish in medical studies that may one day treat or cure heart disease, skin cancer, and muscular dystrophy.

PET FISH

Ichthyologists are not the only people who like to watch fish. Fish are one of the most popular pets that people keep in their homes. Goldfish, guppies, and bettas are easy to care for and fun to watch. Koi, a type of carp, come in many beautiful colors and are often kept in ponds in backyards or in parks. Many people set up an aquarium, a special glass tank, which can hold several types of fish. Home aquariums may hold as little as 1 gallon (3.8 liters) of water

VOCABULARY

Ichthyologists are scientists who study fish.

Koi may be a solid color or have up to three different colors.

or more than 100 gallons (3,785 l)!

Large public aquariums help people learn about fish and their habitats. Most aquariums have many different kinds of fish from different parts of the world. Some have underwater tunnels that let people see fish swim around and above them. Many aquariums have tide pool exhibits or small tanks that allow visitors to touch some types of fish.

Some aquariums are large enough to hold a whale shark, along with many smaller species of fish.

Major Threats to Fish

Human activity can cause major damage to fish populations. When people build dams on rivers the flow of water in the rivers is lowered. That may prevent fish from swimming upstream to spawn. Wetlands are filled in to make way for buildings. Sometimes people release fish into areas where that type of fish has never lived before. If the fish have no natural enemies in their new habitat, they can quickly multiply and may wipe out fish that were already living there.

Oil spills kill fish and other sea life.

People dump garbage and sewage into creeks, rivers, ponds, lakes, and oceans. Factories or cities sometimes release harmful chemicals, oil, and other wastes into water. These can poison the fish that live in the water. Global warming is increasing the temperature of Earth's water. The warmer water kills some plants and other organisms that fish eat. Another problem is overfishing. When too many fish of the same species are caught, the species may become extinct.

THINK ABOUT IT

What threats to fish are caused by people? Are there threats that are caused by nature?

Plastic bags, fishing line, and other types of litter kill fish and their food supplies.

How We Can Help Fish

We can help fish by not building new dams and by removing dams that are no longer needed. In some areas, **fish ladders** have been built to help fish move past dams so they can spawn. Protecting wetlands is another way to help protect fish. Many places are working to prevent people from accidentally introducing fish into areas where the fish do not belong.

Fish ladders help salmon and steelhead make it past dams to reach their spawning grounds.

Some fish farms raise endangered fish to release into the wild, instead of as food.

Fish farming helps prevent overfishing of some species. Some types of fish, such as trout, can be easily bred in captivity. Once hatched, they are raised in tanks or ponds. The grown fish are then sold for food.

Preventing oil spills and other forms of pollution will help keep ocean fish healthy. Some countries are working to stop global warming. This will help keep our rivers and oceans from becoming too warm for fish.

THE WONDERFUL WORLD OF FISH

Fish may be the oldest vertebrates in the world, but we still have a lot to learn about them. New species of fish are discovered every year. Some fish, like the tiny mandarin dragonet, are beautiful. Others, such as piranhas and anglerfish, are scary-looking. Fish live in streams, in rivers, and even in pools in dark underground caves. They live in sunny

COMPARE AND CONTRAST

Compare and contrast the ways fish are like people.

Swimming in a school helps fish protect themselves and find food more easily.

waters and in the deepest part of the ocean where light never reaches.

Some fish live in groups, called schools, to protect themselves from predators. Other fish, like the moray eel, prefer to be alone. No matter what they look like, or where they live, fish are an important part of Earth, and they need our protection.

Mandarin dragonets are some of the most colorful fish in the ocean.

Glossary

aquarium A glass tank in which living water animals or plants are kept.

cold-blooded Having a body temperature that is not regulated by the body.

ecosystem A community of living things interacting with their environment.

fertilize To join the necessary reproductive parts (e.g. a sperm unites with an egg) in order to create life; to increase the likelihood of reproduction or growth.

global warming A warming of Earth's atmosphere and oceans.

larva A young form of an animal that looks very different from its parents.

malaria A fever that is passed on to humans by the bite of mosquitoes.

migrate To move from one place or region to another.

muscular dystrophy An inherited disease that causes increasing weakness of muscles.

plankton Small plants and animals that float or drift in a body of water.

predator An animal that lives by killing and eating other animals.

reproduce To succesfully make new organisms through fertilization, development, and giving birth.

sea anemone A boneless sea animal that looks like a flower and has brightly colored tentacles.

species A group of organisms that have common features and can reproduce young of the same kind.

tropical Having to do with an area that is very warm and wet or humid.

wetlands Lands or areas, such as marshes and swamps, that have much moisture in the soil.

For More Information

Books

De la Bédoyère, Camilla. *My Little Book of Ocean Life*. New York, NY: Scholastic, 2014.

Hamilton, Lynn, and Katie Gillespie. *Caring for My Pet Fish*. New York, NY: AV² by Weigl, 2015.

Marsico, Katie. *Sharks*. New York, NY: Children's Press, 2012.

Rizzo, Johnna. *Ocean Animals: Who's Who in the Deep Blue*. Washington, DC: National Geographic, 2016.

Taylor-Butler, Christine. *Fish*. New York, NY: Scholastic, 2013.

Websites

Because of the changing nature of internet links, Rosen Publishing has developed an online list of websites related to the subject of this book. This site is updated regularly. Please use this link to access this list:

http://www.rosenlinks.com/LFO/fish

Index